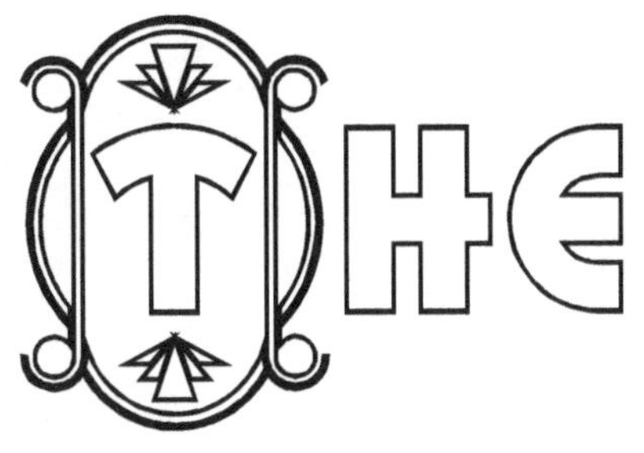

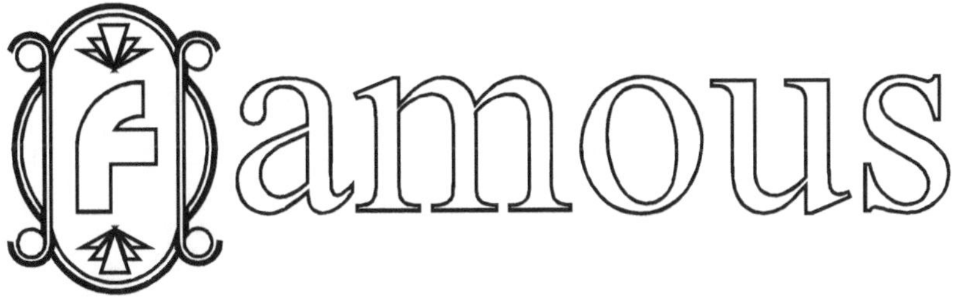

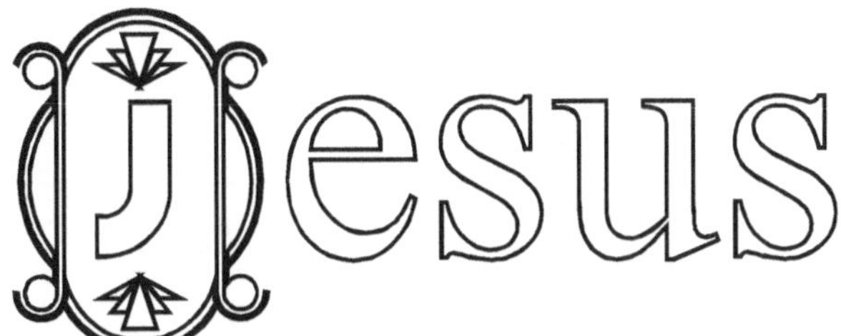

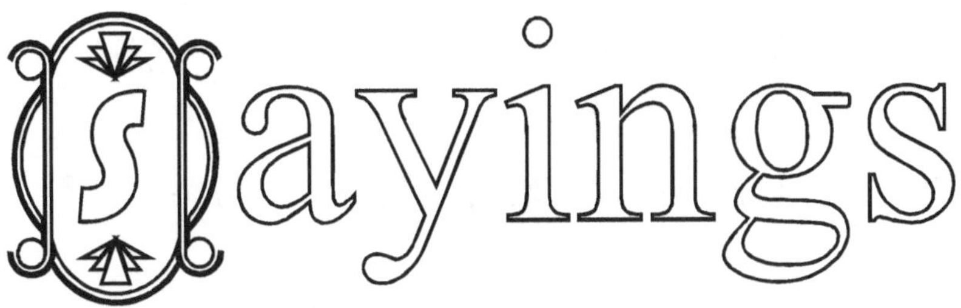

Colouring Book

The Soothing, Simple to Colour Words of Christ

King James Bible Verses

The Famous Jesus Sayings Colouring Book

The Soothing, Simple to Colour Words of Christ

ISBN 978-1-77335-098-1

Magdalene Press, January 2016

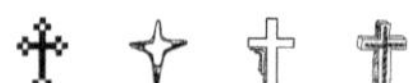

Contents

John 3:16

For God so
loved the world,
that he gave his
only begotten
Son, that
whosoever
believeth in him

should not perish, but have everlasting life.

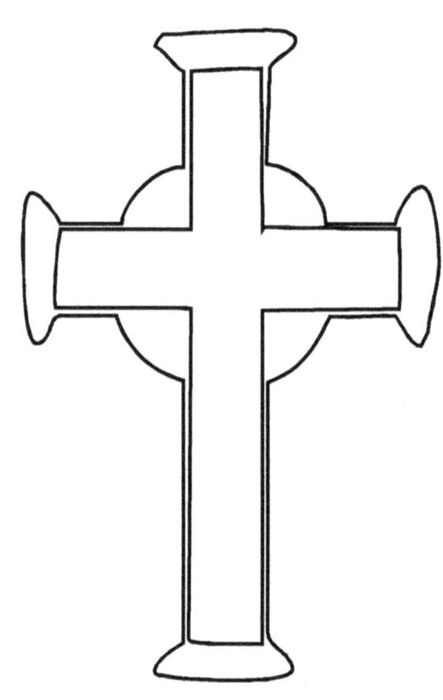

John 10:10, 11

The thief cometh not, but for to steal, and to kill, and to destroy: I am come that they might have life, and that they might have it more abundantly. I am the good shepherd: the good shepherd giveth his life for the sheep.

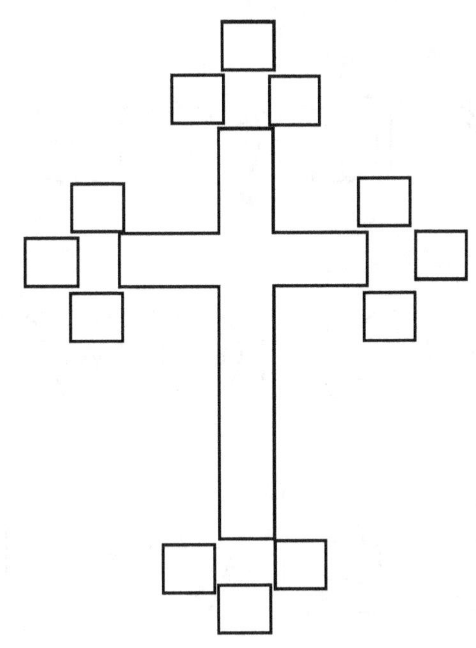

John 10:27-30

My sheep hear
my voice, and I
know them, and
they follow me:
And I give unto
them eternal
life; and they

shall never perish, neither shall any man pluck them out of my hand. My Father, which gave them me, is greater than all; and no man is able to pluck them out of my Father's hand. I and my Father are one.

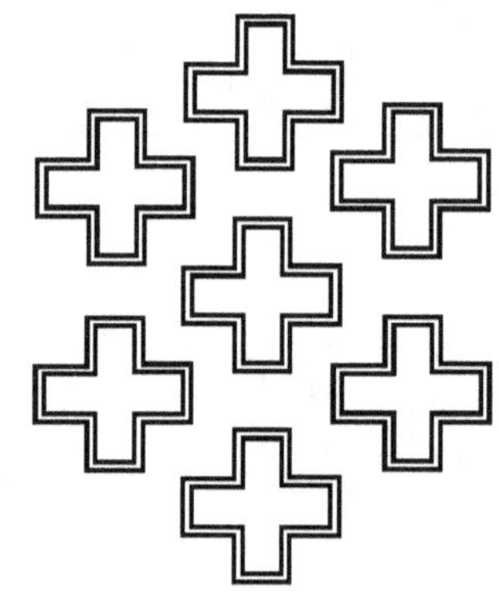

John 14:6

Jesus saith unto him, I am the way, the truth, and the life: no man cometh unto the Father, but by me.

Matthew 6:33

But seek ye first the kingdom of God, and his righteousness; and all these things shall be added unto you.

Matthew 7:7,8

Ask, and it shall be given you; seek, and ye shall find; knock, and it shall be opened unto you: For every one that asketh receiveth; and he that seeketh findeth; and to him that knocketh it shall be opened.

Matthew 19:14

But Jesus said,
Suffer little
children, and
forbid them not,
to come unto
me: for of such

is the kingdom of heaven.

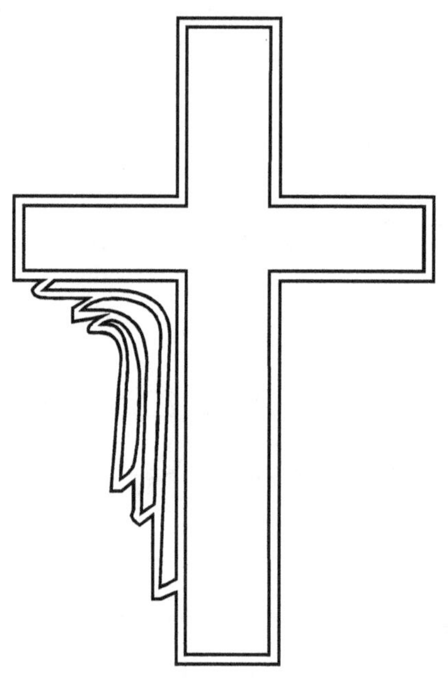

Mark 8:34-37

And when he
had called the
people unto him
with his
disciples also,
he said unto
them,

Whosoever will come after me, let him deny himself, and take up his cross, and follow me. For whosoever will save his life shall lose it; but whosoever shall lose his life for my sake and the gospel's, the same shall save it. For what shall it profit a man, if he shall gain the whole world, and lose his own soul? Or what shall a man give in exchange for his soul?

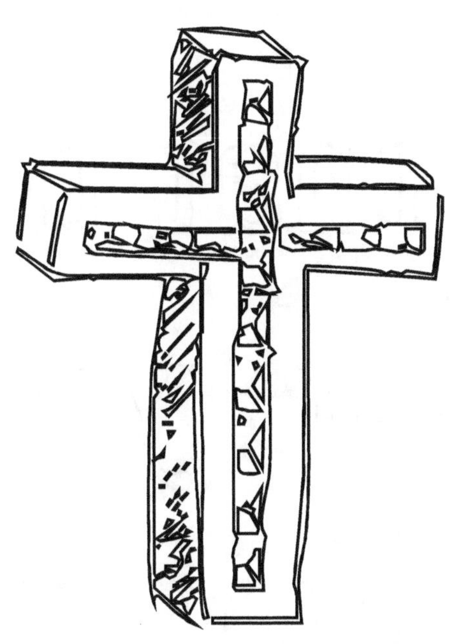

Matthew 5:16

Let your light so shine before men, that they may see your good works, and glorify your

Father which is in heaven.

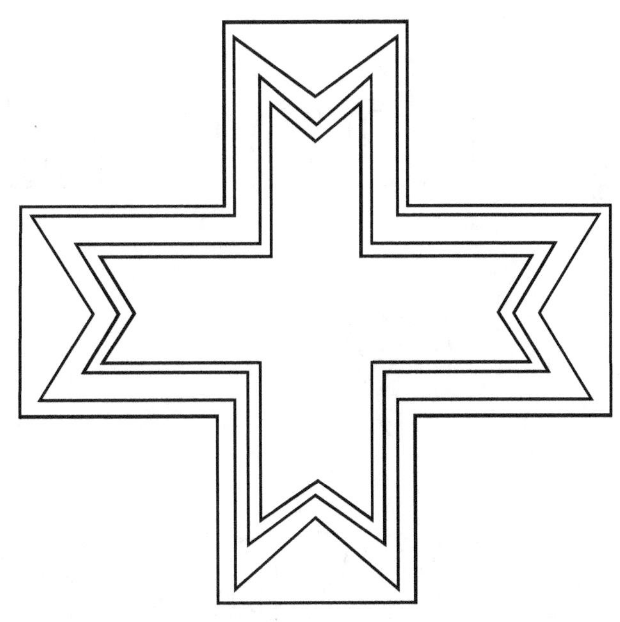

Matthew 5:43-44

Ye have heard that it hath been said, Thou shalt love thy neighbour, and hate thine enemy. But I say unto you, Love your enemies, bless them that curse you, do good to them that hate you, and pray for them which despitefully use you, and persecute you;

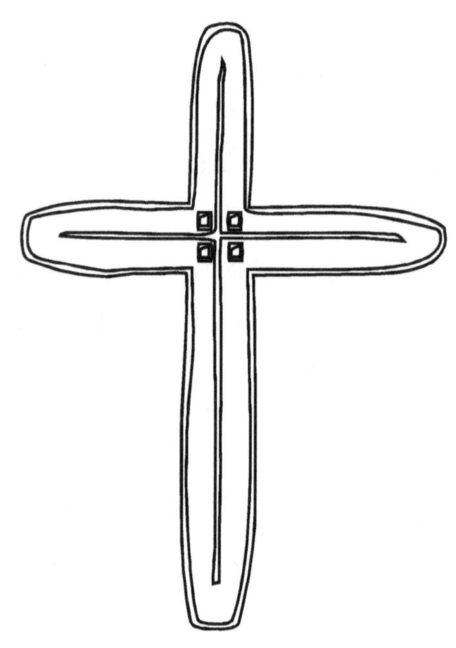

Matthew 7:12

Therefore
all things
whatsoever ye
would that men
should do to
you, do ye even
so to them: for

this is the law and the prophets.

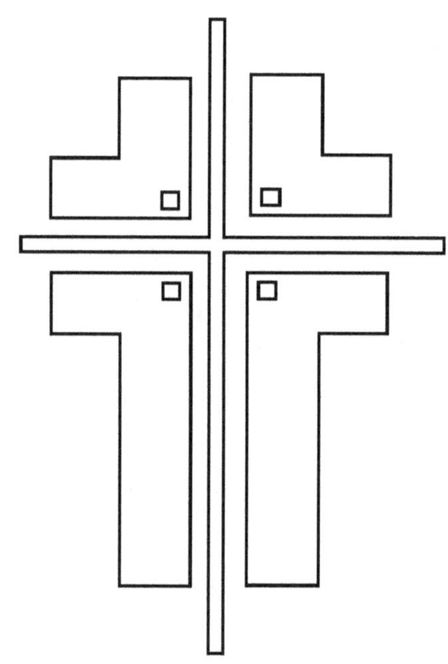

Matthew 22:37-40

Jesus said unto him, Thou shalt love the Lord thy God with all thy heart, and with all thy soul, and with

all thy mind.
This is the first
and great
commandment.
And the second
is like unto it,
Thou shalt love
thy neighbour as

thyself. On these two commandments hang all the law and the prophets.

Mark 10:45

For even the
Son of man
came not to be
ministered unto,
but to minister,
and to give his

life a ransom for many.

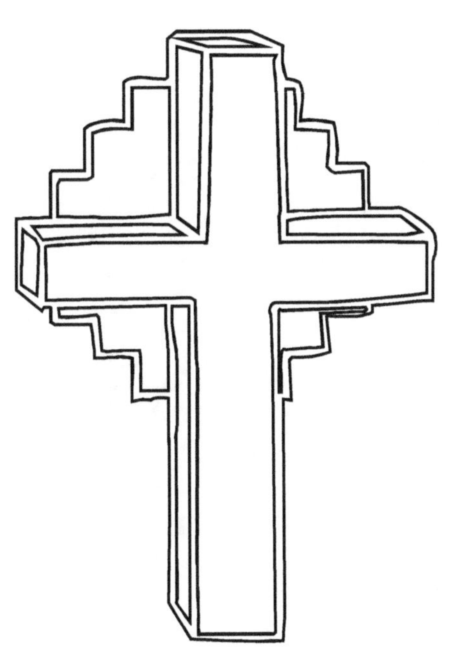

www.ingramcontent.com/pod-product-compliance
Lightning Source LLC
LaVergne TN
LVHW081255100826
845148LV00009B/1226

* 9 7 8 1 7 7 3 3 5 0 9 8 1 *